Cameras
in
Narnia

HOW THE LION, THE WITCH AND THE WARDROBE CAME TO LIFE

Ian Brodie

Foreword by Andrew Adamson

HarperCollinsPublishers

THE CHRONICLES OF NARNIA:
THE LION, THE WITCH AND THE WARDROBE

WALT DISNEY PICTURES AND WALDEN MEDIA PRESENT "THE CHRONICLES OF NARNIA: THE LION, THE WITCH AND THE WARDROBE" BASED ON THE BOOK BY C.S. LEWIS A MARK JOHNSON PRODUCTION AN ANDREW ADAMSON FILM MUSIC COMPOSED BY HARRY GREGSON-WILLIAMS COSTUME DESIGNER ISIS MUSSENDEN EDITED BY SIM EVAN-JONES PRODUCTION DESIGNER ROGER FORD DIRECTOR OF PHOTOGRAPHY DONALD M. McALPINE, ASC, ACS CO-PRODUCER DOUGLAS GRESHAM EXECUTIVE PRODUCERS PHILIP STEUER ANDREW ADAMSON PERRY MOORE SCREENPLAY BY ANN PEACOCK AND ANDREW ADAMSON AND CHRISTOPHER MARKUS & STEPHEN McFEELY PRODUCED BY MARK JOHNSON DIRECTED BY ANDREW ADAMSON

Narnia.com

HarperCollins*Publishers*
77-85 Fulham Palace Road, London W6 8JB
www.harpercollins.co.uk

Published by HarperCollins*Publishers* 2005
1 3 5 7 9 8 6 4 2

ISBN 0 00 721482 0

Cover design by Katy Wright, HarperCollins Design Studio
Designed and typeset by Island Bridge
Printed in China by Phoenix Offset on 128 gsm Matt Art

www.narnia.com

contents

foreword

Andrew Adamson checks a scene before filming using a small viewfinder that mimics the view from a larger movie camera. This allows him to plan the shot before discussing it with the director of photography.

I first read the Narnia Chronicles as an eight-year-old child growing up in Auckland, New Zealand. Narnia has since occupied a special place in my mind as one of the first imaginary worlds that I ever immersed myself in. I read all seven books several times over a couple of years. Little could I have imagined that thirty years later I would be drawing on that eight-year-old's imagination to try and bring Narnia and all its wonderful creatures and characters to the screen. Nor could I have predicted that I would be returning to New Zealand to utilise its landscapes and creative talent to help envision this world.

Film making in New Zealand is not a new thing; we have a rich but modest tradition. Making films on this scale is a much newer experience for this small nation. We were lucky enough to draw on many of the resources Peter Jackson brought together for the *Lord of the Rings* trilogy and take advantage of a fairly newly formed, but highly skilled, work force. It wasn't always this way.

When I left New Zealand in 1991, the film industry as such was minimal. Options for a 'wannabe' film maker were few and far between and few people even realised the potential for working on film. It certainly wasn't taught as any part of a school curriculum or presented as a job option for 'work week' in schools. In fact, learning how films were made would have been almost impossible.

What Ian has done in this book is bring many of the film mysteries, some of which may be taken for granted by film makers, to light. He explains everything from producing to catering, locations to visual effects, all using the making of *The Chronicles of Narnia: The Lion, the Witch and the Wardrobe* as a backdrop.

I hope readers will find information and inspiration within, and through watching the movie be encouraged to look deeper in the world of film making. Perhaps it will propel you, as CS Lewis' books did for me, towards the possibilities of exploring the imagination through the wonderful medium of film.

Andrew Adamson

in the beginning

In 1950 English writer CS Lewis published *The Lion, the Witch and the Wardrobe*, the first of his seven-book series *The Chronicles of Narnia* – the adventures of four children who travel through the back of a wardrobe and into a magical realm. The books have since become classics, loved by children everywhere.

In 1967 and 1988 *The Lion, the Witch and the Wardrobe* was made into a television series, but because of the very basic special effects available at the time, most people found it disappointing. Movie director Andrew Adamson had read and loved the Narnia books as a child and always wanted to make them into movies. In 2002, he was ready to do something about it. By this time, the movie rights were owned by Walden Media, who agreed with him that the time was right to make *The Lion, the Witch and the Wardrobe* into a movie as computer technology and movie-making techniques could now do justice to the fabulous creatures of Narnia.

Movies need someone to organise them and someone to distribute them, and Walt Disney Pictures and Walden Media became production partners for *The Lion, the Witch and the Wardrobe*. Every movie also has to have a budget and for a major motion picture this needs to cover everything from day one of production, including figuring out where they were going to shoot, why and how and over how many days as well as every other physical part of the production.

Everyone knew this was going to be a hugely complex movie and the post-production (work that happens after filming has finished) was going to take a lot of time and money because of the huge amount of computer generation and special effects that would be needed.

When Lucy decided to hide in an old wardrobe, she began a journey into a magical realm, the beginning of an extraordinary adventure . . .

the**director**

Making a movie is like putting together a jigsaw puzzle. Different departments are responsible for their own pieces of the puzzle, but the director is the one who decides what the final movie will look like. The director makes the final decisions on the script, which needed to be adapted from the book by a screenwriter, locations, the shooting schedule and casting. It's a bit like writing a three-dimensional book. While a scene in the book the story comes from may be described in two pages, he has to make it fill the screen with exciting action and be interesting and appealing to an audience that is watching, not reading.

The cast and crew all answer to the director, who works with the producer. The producer answers to the studio and the movie's commercial backers, the people who have financed the movie.

The director decides what is filmed by advising the actors and working with the technical crew. Lighting, camera placement and sound are some of the things this involves. The director also works with the editor in deciding how the film will be put together from all the sequences that have been filmed and then working with the composer and the sound and visual effects teams to complete the movie.

The Lion, the Witch and the Wardrobe was Andrew Adamson's first live action movie. His directing background had been in animated movies (*Shrek* and *Shrek 2*) and these skills were especially important in *The Lion, the Witch and the Wardrobe*. While the movie is live action, almost every scene has something computer generated. It was Andrew's creative interpretation of the story, or how he imagined it, that the actors had to bring to life.

Because the director is involved in every creative part of the film he has to work very long hours. Once everyone else is finished for the day he needs to look at what has been filmed and progress the editing work on the previous few days' filming.

The producer works in partnership with the director to oversee the film, and is the logistical and business manager, making sure the director has everything they need to make the movie within the budget and delivery dates. The producer also has an active role in hiring creative staff, including the cast, director of photography, editor and composer. The producer reports to the studio and the financial backers on how their investment is progressing. *The Lion, the Witch and the Wardrobe* had financial support from two different companies — Walden Media and Disney — and associate producers represented each company.

A particular challenge for Mark Johnson, the producer of *The Lion, the Witch and the Wardrobe*, was working with the complex visual effects necessary to make photo-realistic creatures.

Executive producer Philip Steuer worked with Mark and looked after the physical production of the movie — such as how the budget was managed, when filming moved to another location and how much was spent on things like accommodation and travel. The movie was made in four countries — the United States, New Zealand, England and the Czech Republic, with location scouting and research in Poland and South America.

After filming is completed, the producer works with the director to finish the film with the editors, sound designer, animators and composer. They also work with the marketing and publicity department to promote the movie.

Because the producer has control of the budget they are sometimes put in the difficult position of having to say no — this can happen when the director wants to do something that exceeds the budget or causes problems with the filming schedule.

the producer and executive producer

Above
Producer Mark Johnson: 'I think what I love doing is putting everything together. Making sure the director has all the elements — the crew and a great cast. I like standing back on the set and just watching everybody do their job — it gives me great satisfaction.'

Left
'For a movie of such size, with all kinds of creatures and intricate visual effects, it has been the quiet moments watching Georgie, the girl who plays Lucy, do her scenes with Mr Tumnus that I've enjoyed the most, realising the magic and the poetry is going to come.' Mark Johnson.

what will it
look like?

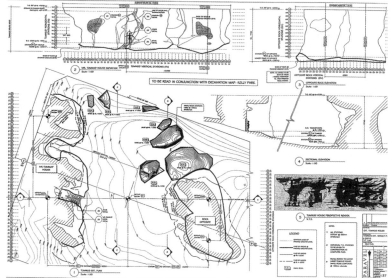

Above right
The contour plan for Mr Tumnus' house and surrounding area, showing the rocks, trees and elevations the pre-vis department used to create the 3D computer set.

Above top
Complicated scenes such as the great battle were constructed in a computer by pre-vis to allow many different camera angles and combinations of shots to be looked at before expensive shooting with an entire production team began. For example — close-up or panning.

Above
While the final movie is a combination of many different components that won't be seen together until a year after filming begins, pre-vis allowed the director and DoP to view and approve in advance a final scene and determine the way they would shoot it when filming started.

Right
Pre-vis supervisor Rpin Suwannath brings the location information, action sequence, camera angles and the director's vision together in his computer. Here he is working on a scene from the great battle where Peter is fighting the White Witch.

Movies used to start with storyboards — when artists showed the main scenes and action sequences as a series of drawings. While this was a very useful way of helping the director to decide how the movie would look, modern computer technology has found a much more effective way to 'imagine' the movie.

This is called pre-visualisation, or pre-vis. Pre-vis is like a virtual movie, where ideas are tested before the cameras roll. Movies cost millions of dollars to make so being able to work ideas out beforehand is very useful and saves a lot of time and money. Pre-vis also allows the director and the director of photography (DoP) to be more creative — they can try something twenty different ways before they start filming. In a movie like *The Lion, the Witch and the Wardrobe*, many of the scenes are very complex, with real actors combining with computer-generated characters and some that are a combination of both, with special effects added to scenes shot on location. Pre-vis provides a structure for what can be very complicated sequences, so the director can check that everything that needs to be covered has been included in a scene. This means that when filming starts, the team know that technically everything will work. Without pre-vis, people can plan

something and not find out until they're on the set that it isn't going to
work so they have to compromise, which can be expensive.

Once a location has been chosen, a surveying team maps out the
area — right down to the placement of individual rocks and trees, and
this information is sent to the pre-vis team.

The director discusses his ideas with the pre-vis supervisor, who
creates computer images of the characters with the animators, who
begin to 'tell' the story in animated form. This allows the director to
try out different ideas and camera angles so he can 'see' what they will
look like in the movie and decide on the best options. A team of seven
animators worked on *The Lion, the Witch and the Wardrobe*.

At the same time, the art department are designing sets, where
the action and scenes will be filmed. The physical measurements and
dimensions of the set are mapped out and provided to the pre-vis team,
who combine the set information and the location information to make
an accurate three-dimensional computer model where ideas can be
tried out — a bit like a video game.

The pre-vis for *The Lion, the Witch and the Wardrobe* began in
March 2002, more than two years before filming started, and ended in
December 2004. Director Andrew Adamson and pre-vis supervisor Rpin
Suwannath sat down with the script and Andrew described the sorts
of creatures he wanted to see in the film, and how each scene should
look.

The pre-vis supervisor also discusses the sorts of cameras the DoP is
going to use, and using the computer model and 3D set, he 'flies' the
cameras through the set and looks at it from lots of different angles to
see which one works the best. By the time pre-vis was finished, Andrew
and the DoP had a better idea of how they were going to film the movie
and where to place the cameras and refined the script. The machines
pre-vis use are like word processors for movies, and are a whole new
storytelling technique which lets the director write the script visually.

Tools for pre-vis

- Work station or computer
- Powerful 3D software package
- Editing software
- Skilled 3D animators

Pre-vis jargon

- *Cut scenes:* individual scenes that make up the story
- *Animatics:* joining the cut scenes to make a sequence
- *Blocking:* simple animation to show the basic elements and features in a scene, not fully animated
- *Layering:* building up a 3D image in layers so you can 'look' through a wall to see what would be on the other side, or see into a house or behind a rock

casting
— *choosing the actors*

Scottish actress Tilda Swinton was cast in the leading adult role of the White Witch. As well as being a talented actress, she had the strong, clean beauty needed to play the extraordinary character.

Because the four children in the story were English, Pippa Hall travelled up and down the United Kingdom visiting schools, drama groups, youth centres, theatres and acting agencies. She said: 'The read through for this film was an amazing experience. William, Anna, Skandar and Georgie all sat down at the table and were just themselves — it was perfect, it just worked so well. Everyone else in the room kept looking at each other gobsmacked. We all felt so good after that.'

Casting is the process of choosing the actors. For *The Lion, the Witch and the Wardrobe* there were two casting directors. Pippa Hall cast the children who played Peter, Susan, Edmund and Lucy in England and Liz Mullane cast the New Zealanders who played other characters and extras. Most of the adult roles, including voices for animal characters, were cast by Pippa Hall and Gail Stevens.

Casting directors begin by reading the script and researching the physical characteristics of each character, and the acting range each role needs. Before they start they also find out what the director has in mind, as he will make the final decision.

For *The Lion, the Witch and the Wardrobe*, Pippa Hall knew the children needed to look as if they were brothers and sisters. She also knew what sort of emotions they would need to be able to show and what sort of things they would need to do — including riding horses and fighting with swords and bows and arrows.

The children who tried out for *The Lion, the Witch and the Wardrobe* had to read through scenes and do a film test so the director could see how they would look on the screen. Thousands of children were auditioned and 2000 girls tried out for the role of Lucy, which went to Georgie Henley. The role of Edmund went to Skandar Keynes.

It was late at night when Andrew Adamson made his final decision, saying he would call the children in the morning. Because Pippa knew the older two would still be awake, she persuaded him to call straight away. William Moseley, who played Peter, was stunned when he heard the news and when Andrew said to Anna Popplewell 'Would you like to be Susan?' she was so excited she screamed down the phone.

choosing **locations**

This board illustrates the many hours the location team spent photographing and mapping each location to allow all the other departments to gain the working knowledge of the set area they would need to plan their own part in the filming process.

Some of the scenes in a movie are filmed inside a studio, but some need to be filmed outside, on location, and the locations department have to find places that match the director's vision of a particular scene or sequence.

The person responsible for this is the supervising location manager, who usually starts their search a long time before filming starts, by calling in local experts and doing research. This can involve reading books and looking at maps and topographical information. When they have a list of possible locations, they visit each one and take photographs and detailed measurements. These are presented to the director, the DoP and the producers. Choices are made and the location supervisor organises a scouting trip to the location. If the director says this is it, they can stop looking — if not, the search continues.

Once a location is chosen, the location supervisor has to organise everything necessary to make it happen. This can mean negotiation with the land owner, getting all the legal permits they will need and working out the logistics of getting the cast and the technical crew in and out of the location. The location team has to build the base camp where filming will take place — and when the location is in a remote area this can mean everything from building roads and bringing in power generators and water supplies to providing helipads, shelter tents and rain covers, sanitation facilities including portable toilets and massive tents for storing costumes and props. They also need to provide signs and maps for the cast, crew and any visitors to the set.

The location crew have to maintain everything at the location and base camp while filming is under way, and once it's finished, they have to break it all down again. Then they have to restore the site back to its original condition.

Because *The Lion, the Witch and the Wardrobe* is a fantasy, with mythical creatures like fauns, centaurs, cyclops and Minotaurs, thirty make-up stations were needed, all needing running water, electricity, special mirrors and strengthened seats and benches for the giants, who were all over two metres tall and weighed more than 180 kg.

Above top
James Crowley and his team used a wide variety of resources and means of transportation to scout for locations in a number of countries.

Above
Flock Hill, in Canterbury, was the location for the great battle. The base camp and 6 km access road were built at the lowest part of the site so it wouldn't be visible from where they were filming. A bridge was constructed to access the site and three major locations were used from the base camp, including one accessible only by helicopter. The base camp was like a small town, with medical staff, and catering for over 600 people over six weeks of intensive filming.

creating the
sets

Above right
The skills of the art department created the imaginary interior of Mr Tumnus' house.

Above top
Many books and images of the 1940s were used to obtain the exact style of the times to create the interior of the Professor's house. Exterior shots were taken in other places and then added to the interiors shot at Hobsonville.

Above
The huge snow set at Kelly Park north of Auckland was used to create many winter scenes of Narnia. The snow and cheery lights in the window create a perfect illusion of the Beavers' dam.

Once the script is finalised, the production designer, who heads the art department, joins the creative team along with the director and DoP. Roger Ford was the production designer for *The Lion, the Witch and the Wardrobe* and the creative team spent three months on pre-pre-production, deciding how the film would look. This involved early concept work and pre-visualisation, including how the make-up, hair and costumes needed to look, especially the colours and styles, to make sure the actors would look right in every scene.

Movies are filmed or shot on sets, which are constructed either in a studio or outside on location. *The Lion, the Witch and the Wardrobe* was a complicated project with 75 sets built in three countries — New Zealand, England and the Czech Republic. The story needed sets designed for dismal wartime London, the Professor's house in the English countryside and then the fantasy land of Narnia, each with a very different look.

From there the movie moved into pre-production, employing an art department of thirty to continue work on the set design, before a construction team was employed to build the sets. For *The Lion, the Witch and the Wardrobe*, this meant everything from the silk tents in Aslan's camp to the Beavers' dam and Cair Paravel.

One very special prop was the old wooden wardrobe the children used to enter Narnia, which Andrew Adamson decided should tell the story of *The Magician's Nephew*, the first book in the Chronicles of Narnia, in the carvings on its doors.

If the production designer was the architect for the movie, then the supervising art director, Ian Gracie, was the builder. He oversaw everything from concept through to draughting plans, writing engineering specifications and the building, painting and sculpting for all the sets. He also needed to check that everything was working and looking right all through filming.

For each set, the art department made a detailed model, and once it had the creative team's approval it was created in 3D in the computer, so the pre-vis team could add it to the location information and begin to use it while the set was being built.

Movies can be made using partial set pieces — this means you don't have to build huge sets to show the background of a scene; you just build the working part and computer-generate the rest later. But if you do it this way, you need to make sure it has been designed correctly so that when the computer-generated part is added the light comes in the windows from the correct angle and the elements all fit together smoothly.

The set must be ready when the director starts filming, it has to have cost the right amount of money and it has to be practical — it's no use having a great-looking set if you can't get the camera in where it needs to be to capture the action the way the director wants.

Sometimes a particular scene has an interior and an exterior view, such as the Beavers' dam. These might be built in two completely different places, but the lighting and the camera angles need to match. When there are several sets on the same sound stage the art department needs to make sure there is enough room for the cameras and cranes to move smoothly between them.

The carving of the apple tree in the centre of the wardrobe door is a clue to the identity of the Professor. He is Digory, the young boy who brought an apple back from Narnia to cure his dying mother many years before. The wardrobe which transports the children to Narnia is made of wood from the apple tree that grew when he planted the core.

Nearing completion — the courtyard of the White Witch's castle with the frozen statues of her victims in place.

The construction manager who supervised building the sets and some of the larger props for *The Lion, the Witch and the Wardrobe* was Greg Hajdu, who was responsible for the sets being ready on time, and for breaking them all down once filming was complete. He employed a construction crew of over 250 carpenters, plasterers, painters, steelworkers and sculptors.

As well as the structures in each location, the construction crew also had to build the area around them, from frozen landscapes to the White Witch's castle and two very different camps at the site of the great battle — Aslan's and the White Witch's.

One of the hardest tasks was creating the Witch's icy courtyard, main hall and dungeon out of fibreglass, so that it looked translucent. It was made in huge sections and because no one had ever done that before, the team had to work out how to do it for themselves.

Sets are only built to last for the period of filming so they are made from plywood and other light materials which are easier to manoeuvre and transport. However, they also need to look convincing. Castle walls that look as if they're made of stone may in fact be carved from polystyrene and the floors of Cair Paravel used one and a half kilometres of vinyl made to look like marble by photographing the real thing and printing it onto the vinyl.

Modern technology has also simplified the carpenters' job. A computer-controlled CNC router can be programmed to cut all the components for a set in the correct sizes and shapes so that the carpenters can assemble them like a huge jigsaw puzzle.

Above

Detailed plans provided by the art department allowed set builders to manufacture the many sets as quickly as possible. As one was pulled down another was ready to be assembled.

Below right

Heavy equipment is run into the set on specially laid tracks to avoid damaging any part of the set. As all the pieces are assembled like a large jigsaw the many metres of vinyl 'marble' are laid over the top.

Below and opposite

The original design for the White Witch's throne, and how it appeared in the movie.

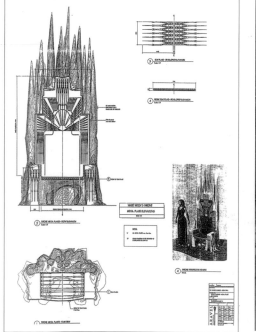

The manufacture of these weapons is only the first part of their journey. They then have to be shipped to set and carefully placed by the set decorators.

arming *and* equipping
Narnia

Discussions with Richard Taylor of Weta Studios began two years before filming started, with Weta producing a broad range of illustrations to pin down exactly how Narnia looked, as they would be involved in designing and making various props, jewellery, costuming, armour, weapons and 3D maquettes (small one-sixth scale sculptures of principal characters and their environment). Once they were approved, larger maquettes were made and scanned by the visual effects department to obtain accurate data for the creation of the digital creatures.

Because CS Lewis didn't describe the physical details of Narnia and its creatures in great detail in his books, there was no detailed reference to work from that would tell the design team the sorts of things they would need to know to make Narnia come to life. Andrew and Richard and the various design teams had to invent a culture for Narnia and Weta made early landscape and architectural designs including environments, costuming, armour and weapons. At the same time Andrew assembled a team of concept artists in America to work with him and twice-weekly video conferences kept both teams in touch.

Once the look of Narnia and the types of creatures had been agreed, Weta began the huge task of arming the two great armies that would battle for control of the kingdom.

The principal weapons were swords and daggers, from the centaurs' great broadswords to the Minotaurs' distinctive blades and Peter's smaller sword. Movie swords come in three varieties — hero swords for the main characters and close-ups, stunt-fighting swords, which need to be strong enough for real action, and background swords for the extras, which only need to look the part.

The Lion, the Witch and the Wardrobe needed 28 hero swords, which were hand ground out of block spring steel then acid etched — exactly how a real sword is made. If they were sharpened they could cut off someone's head. They were very heavy and skilled craftspeople took between two and seven months to make each weapon.

Stunt swords have their handgrip and crossbar made from skateboard wheel rubber, painted to look like the real thing, with aluminium blades so they are lighter and easier to handle. Because they are being used in live action they have a slightly softer edge so they won't split the skin if someone is accidentally hit.

Another safety concern on set is that real armour is very dangerous to wear. If an actor falls and the armour crushes you can't easily bend it out again to remove them from it. The biggest danger is for men — you only have to fall on your knees for the impact to drive the chest plate into the Adam's apple, which can be fatal.

Because much of the armour had to be made for non-human creatures with hooves, animal-like back legs and interesting chests, the designers had to think about how these four-legged animals would carry themselves once they stood upright. The Minotaurs carry very heavy extravagant armour which shows their arrogance, so a lot of design work went into getting this look right.

The background swords were made from urethane with a slightly thicker blade and a piece of wire down the middle to stop them wobbling. They were painted to look realistic and unless you touch or bend them it's almost impossible to tell them from the real thing.

Above top
Just as in medieval times, Stu Johnston hand beats steel with the aid of a hammer and anvil to create armour that not only looks right but could also be worn in battle.

Above
The craftsmanship of Weta — even at very close range these belts look as if they were crafted in Narnia many years ago.

Left
A team of manufacturers at Weta Studios in Wellington spent many hours with angle grinders removing the flashing from the armour, preparing it for painting and having the various webbing attached.

Body armour was made by a team of 100 craftspeople, and they used hand-beaten steel, exactly as it was made in medieval times. They made beautiful armour using three basic tools — a block of wood, a ballpen hammer and a sheet of steel. The armour was then polished with electric buffers. Because this armour is very heavy it was only used for close-ups. Copies of the armour were made with box silicon moulds using flexible urethane, light enough for the actors to wear while filming. Once the silicon armour comes out of the mould the rough edges have to be ground off. This took a dozen people ten hours a day for ten months to make all the armour for the extras.

Then a whole army of people assembled the pieces — the flexible armour came through the painting shop and had colour applied to make it look like real steel, leather or wood. It had to be almost indestructible because it can't be scratched or broken while being worn, so each piece was painted with a special substance called volchem which bites through the surface of the paint and into the urethane. Once it dries not even a car key will scratch the surface. Thousands of individual components were put together in the assembly room. Keeping track of them was a huge job because every culture (Minotaur, Centaur, Faun) had its own type of armour.

Above top
Tools of the trade with the results in the background. The many detailed sketches provided the craftspeople with all the information they needed to create these works of art.

Above
Defining the cultures of Narnia with heraldry and motifs that would work on all items of clothing, weapons and swords was a major task for Weta Studios.

Right above
The head of Weta, Richard Taylor, visits the set to check all is working smoothly with his creations.

Right below
A walk around Weta Studios in Wellington is an amazing experience, watching hundreds of dedicated experts creating cultures and their related artefacts literally from their heads and hands.

Left top

Sword master Peter Lyon hand buffs the wooden hilt of a hero sword. He has years of experience both in making and using these types of weapons.

Far left centre

Chain mail is made from plastic, otherwise the weight would be unbearable. Each individual link is manually joined to the next — their creation keeping people occupied for many months.

Far left bottom

Helmets lined up on set ready for the extras. The Weta tent on set was enormous, and provided a whole environment for dressing and arming the extras.

Left bottom

As well as making the weapons, Weta provided experts, including Robert Gillies, one of three lead stand-bys. He dressed the main characters in their armour and looked after their swords. During filming he looked out for any scratches, marks or defects that might give the game away that the swords and armour weren't always made of steel. The Weta team also made any repairs.

Altogether Weta made 1200 swords and other weapons, 200 sets of armour including helmets, shields and a large number of props. Along with scabbards, they also made buckles, belts, catches, webbing for the armour and leatherwork, with specially designed insignias stamped into the leather. Because everything had to fit the actors perfectly, there were lots of fittings and adjustments. At the same time Weta also had to interact with the director, the wardrobe department and the creatures department to make sure everything worked and looked right.

When all that was done, the characters were labelled, numbered, hung on racks and bagged after being given a final check before they were packed into containers or trucks to make the final journey to location. Once there Weta had to maintain them, with a specialist team looking after the day-to-day dressing of characters and extras, maintenance of equipment on set, including any running repairs or colour adjustments the director might want.

Once the cameras are ready to roll and the lead actor is on set in full battle armour a buzz of excitement goes around the crew — it's all beginning to look real.

Specialty props from Weta

- Turkish delight bowls
- Goblets
- Queen Susan's jewellery and dagger
- White Witch's wand and dagger
- Ceremonial horns
- Lucy's vial

In total, the Weta team spent 337,500 hours working on props and armour for *The Lion, the Witch and the Wardrobe* — the same time it would have taken them to build 135 houses!

dressing
witches, centaurs
and queens

The costume design team were very creative, brilliant, inspired people who gave 120 per cent and were always bringing up new ideas. Because they had studied around the world and had years of experience there wasn't a problem they weren't able to solve. More than sixty people were involved in the detailed work of making the costumes.

Above top

The personality of the White Witch is transformed in the course of the film. The clever use of costume changes and different styles reflect this.

Above

Running repairs are often necessary on set. Day-to-day wear involving climbing rocks takes its toll.

The costume designer for *The Lion, the Witch and the Wardrobe* was Isis Mussenden, who was responsible for everything the actors wear in the movie — from head to toe. Her job began by reading the script, and then working with the director and actors to help to visually tell the story he had in mind through the clothes the characters wear.

A colour palette (range of colours) for the film was decided with the production designer, lighting designer and DoP. The costume design had to deal with the actors' skin tones and colours, because actors who look good in one colour might not look so good in another. The costume designer tries to stay within the palette the art department has decided for the movie and various scenes to maintain a consistent look and mood. The costume designer also works closely with the art director so that the costumes match and complement the visual style of the sets.

The Lion, the Witch and the Wardrobe had two completely different sorts of costumes — the first part of the movie needed historically accurate clothes from the 1940s and the rest for the fantasy world of Narnia. Isis began researching — she read the book over and over again, and books written about Narnia, as well as looking in the childhood museum of the Victoria and Albert in London, where she went through the archives to see how clothing was stitched, what type of fabrics and buttons were used and what colours they were. Everything had to be made, from the shoes to socks to underwear. Fabric was woven for Lucy and Susan's coats and Peter and Edmund's pants, to match the weaves and designs of the time. A common fabric used in the 1940s was vyella, a mix of wool and cotton, and Isis and her team had to search around the world for it.

Isis often uses paintings as inspiration and refers to them for ideas about pattern and style. She started with the underwear, and every single piece of clothing was specially made. Some items were woven in New York, shoes were made in Australia and cloaks made on authentic antique looms by Stansborough Fabrics in Wellington.

The costumes for Narnia were much more difficult, especially for the White Witch, who was half giant and not quite human. She needed to be beautiful, cold, mean and gorgeous — all at the same time. The designs for her all came from the imagery of ice and Isis and her team started playing with fabrics and colour and storyline to decide her final look. Once Tilda had been cast, they could begin to make her spectacular costumes.

For the White Witch's amazing white dress, a special kind of lace was created from raw silk and raw merino wool which was coloured and felted, then stitched and partly burned out to create what the costume designers called 'witch lace'. Throughout the movie, the White Witch has six different costumes that mirror her character's changing story through colour and shape. The White Witch was increasingly brutal and irreverent towards the creatures of Narnia as her story unfolded, which is something Isis has highlighted in the costumes she designed for Tilda to wear. Her first costume was inspired by snow and ice, and as spring begins to come to Narnia, this begins to change.

Isis also had to create costumes for all the creatures and it was decided she should use tones of gold and red for the goodies and blues with deep blacks and singed colours for the baddies.

For the coronation at Cair Paravel, the art department had chosen a neoclassical look with a summer colour palette, and Isis chose patterns for each of the children's coronation robes that would look good in this setting. She based Lucy's dress on laurel leaves and flowers, and Susan's on daffodils printed with gold leaf on a pale blue background.

Above top
As well as clothing, careful attention was paid to the White Witch's icicle crown. During the thawing of Narnia and the weakening of her power, the icicles slowly melt.

Above
Once each garment was completed it was wrapped and carefully taken to set.

Left
Inspiration for the costume designs comes from paintings, photos and sketches as well as the designer's imagination!

getting the look right
— make-up in Narnia

Above
Lights and heat can affect the way an actor's face looks on screen. Nikki Gooley softens Peter's skin tones to achieve a natural look.

Below
The make-up area is a hive of activity from 4.00 a.m. each morning as the team paint, touch up and blow dry each extra.

The make-up and hair supervisor has to have every character looking exactly right in front of the cameras, and the make-up and hair supervisor for *The Lion, the Witch and the Wardrobe* was Nikki Gooley. Her job started with organising make-up tests for the actors and designing, styling and creating the look for each character. To do this she had to read the script and then meet with the actors, director, production and costume designers and collaborate with all of them so that everything came together smoothly when filming started.

One of the things she needed to think about was how the children's skin colouring would need to change. When the movie starts they are in wartime England, looking very pale but when spring arrives in Narnia they need to gradually become healthier looking. On the other hand, the White Witch had to look pale and icy throughout, and her make-up was difficult to keep looking perfect.

One of the hardest parts of the job is maintaining characters' make-up over a long shoot, keeping it looking natural and not letting it build up too much during the course of the day. This is especially difficult when filming outside on location, where the make-up team have to deal with sunburn, windburn and rain.

The make-up supervisor also needs to work closely with the DoP to make sure the actors' skin tones look right when seen through the camera, or to fix any tiny blemishes that might be showing in a close-up. For the outdoor scenes, some of which were shot in bright sunshine, the actors also had to use lots of sunscreen.

Above left
To the untrained eye all make-up looks perfect but there is always something to be retouched to achieve the desired result.

Above right
Make-up is initially applied in the make-up trailer but is then touched up between each take to ensure continuity.

Far left
The natural skin tones of Tilda Swinton were used to advantage — her pale skin only needed subtle touches.

Left
As the set can be quite some distance from base camp, each make-up artist must carry all they will need during the day, attached to special belts. Sometimes a ladder might have also been handy.

Below
Cuts and bruises are carefully applied to Edmund. All the team on set are connected to each other by radio telephone so they know timings and when the actor will be required to shoot the next take.

Hair and wigs were also part of Nikki's responsibility, and there were some spectacular wigs for the White Witch, whose appearance changed several times during the movie. Anna Popplewell, who played Susan, had hair extensions to make her hair look longer while William Moseley's hair was coloured to make it look blonder in Peter's springtime scenes. Because Georgie Henley's hair was quite dark they added blonde streaks to help with the contrasts for Lucy's final look.

As well as working in the main make-up tents, Nikki and her team took mobile make-up kits with foundations and powders onto the set, and they had a lot of fun putting dirt and scratches on Skandar Keynes, the actor who played Edmund. Each day lots of reference photos were taken and detailed notes marked up in a continuity book in case any scene had to be reshot later on and the actors needed to be made up to look exactly the same.

meet the production team

Above top
With a workforce of over 500 people, each day of shooting comes at a significant cost.

Above
The Lion, the Witch and the Wardrobe had two units working to obtain all the footage they needed in the time that had been allowed for filming. Both were using cranes that are expensive to rent and operate in sometimes awkward or remote locations.

The production department, overseen by executive producer Philip Steuer, has to keep track of all the money that has been allocated for the movie, and the production managers, Beth DePatie and Tim Coddington, who monitored each individual departmental budget, needed to know how to use that money wisely. They reported on a weekly basis to the producer and director, so Mark and Andrew always knew how much had been spent when they were making decisions about how many extras to use on a particular day or how much they had to spend if they needed to get a crane on location.

The production managers help them with these decisions by knowing things like the fact that a crane costs the same amount as 25 extras for a day, or an additional hour of shooting. Every time you choose to spend money on a movie set, you are choosing not to spend money on something else, so they needed to keep Andrew informed so he could make the best decisions. They also needed to be able to estimate accurately, and know, for example, how much the wolves were going to cost for the rest of the movie, so the director could say 'I don't know if I want to spend that much money on real wolves, I'd prefer to spend that money on 20 more ogres.'

To be able to do this the production managers need to know how each department works, what they need and know what that costs from experience.

There was a moment long before production started, when Beth found herself in northern Poland on the border with Belarus, photographing sticks beavers had chewed, for research for the art department that didn't exist yet. It was freezing and she was completely bundled up taking close-up pictures of little beaver marks and thought 'What am I doing? This is weird!'

The other production manager, New Zealander Tim Coddington, used his local knowledge to guide the production through local protocols, customs and ways of doing things and, as he put it, 'turn the money into things, and make things fit for the money — locations, people, places, keeping everything on track and target what the producers and the director want. Everybody's job on the film set is as important as the next person's. We've got a director who has a wonderful vision and he can articulate that vision to everybody. It's one of those films where you come on board and you have to share that vision. There's room for input, but there's no room to be pushing a different vision, and there's no room for guesswork.'

Above
As the cameras capture the scenes, the production team are continually monitoring actual costs against budget.

Below left
The director checks a scene with the DoP. Ensuring this team have all the tools they need to make the film is also an important part of the production team's role.

Below right
Production manager Beth DePatie watches progress as the splinter unit film Narnia in spring at Paradise, near Queenstown in the South Island of New Zealand.

cameras
in Narnia

The Director of Photography (DoP) for *The Lion, the Witch and the Wardrobe* was Don McAlpine, who was responsible for all the camera operators. Also known as the cinematographer, the DoP has to capture on film the director's vision of each scene. Each day, the director and the DoP start with nothing more than ideas or pre-vis, and have to turn all of that into a tangible moving picture. The challenge is to visually interpret each scene onto a screen in an interesting, exciting or evocative way.

The DoP has to understand the principles of photography and appreciate what colours can achieve. For example a blue light can suggest night in one situation, and sadness in another. The DoP needs to know which colour will be appropriate for each situation or scene.

The Lion, the Witch and the Wardrobe was an interesting project to film because of the way it mixes computer-generated and live characters, and one of the challenges was to fit the two together seamlessly.

When a scene is being shot, there can be up to four different cameras recording the action. The main camera is the A camera, and for *The Lion, the Witch and the Wardrobe* the A camera operator was Peter McCaffrey. Put very simply, his job was to make sure his camera was pointed in the right direction at precisely the right time to film exactly what the director and the DoP want in each shot.

In between moments of intense concentration and long periods of waiting, the next scene is set up. The B camera team with Don McAlpine.

Camera talk

- *'Check the gate'*: instruction from the director at the end of a shot, a way to let people know the shot is complete. The aperture of the camera is behind a pressure plate that swings like a gate. The first assistant opens the gate and makes sure there is no foreign matter from hair to sticks to insects and no scratching on the film.

- *Key light*: the main source of light for a scene or subject

- *Boom shot*: shot taken from a moving boom using different camera levels and angles

- *Cutaway*: a shot related to the main action that cuts away briefly and then returns

- *Long shot*: a shot in which the subject is seen from a distance

- *Pan shot*: a shot in which the camera moves horizontally around a fixed axis from one part of a scene to another

- *Reverse angle shot*: a shot in which the angle is the opposite to that in the shot before — used to alternate between two characters' points of view

Each shot is set up in the camera so the director and DoP can look in the monitor and decide if it's what they want, or if they want to adjust the height or angle to improve the shot. How high the camera is above the ground is important and the camera operator also talks to the art department and might ask them to move a flag because it looks as if it's sticking out of an actor's head, for example. The camera operators also have to work in with props and lighting and the boom operator, so that nothing appears in the frame that shouldn't be there.

The camera operator's day starts with a call sheet so they know what's coming up, and they look at the pre-vis to see what they will be shooting. Usually a scene starts with a master shot, a wide-angle shot that shows what everyone is going to do in that scene. This tells the operator an actor is going to walk along this line and go over there. The scene is mapped out in the master shot, and marks put on the ground for the actors and the camera to aim for. They practise taking the camera in and reversing out again several times until they find the perfect position. Sometimes a hand-held viewfinder is used for this part to save moving the heavy camera around. A decision is made about which camera and which lens will be used — and if it will need a tripod or a dolly. Dollies can only move up and down about four feet, so if the camera needs to go any higher it needs a crane.

Above
Four cameras capture a scene at Flock Hill. One is hidden behind the screen while the small hand unit is being used for the 'Making Of' documentary. It took some considerable effort to lift the camera to the top of the ladder for this special shot.

Left
Alfie Speight carefully hovers his helicopter above the rocks as the space cam focuses on the stunt stand-in. A difficult shot that demands total concentration from all involved.

Above
While the camera and boom were capturing the image, the operator and focus puller were in a tent over 200 metres away operating the camera via remote control. Two grips operate the boom, one manually shifting the unit while the other controls the length of the extension with remotes. All the team are connected via radio.

Below left
The modern film camera uses quite old technology. A claw comes around and drags the film down as the shutter spins and exposes the film. This has happened since the first motion picture camera was invented and although it is now refined with computer control and uses much better film stock and lenses, it is still basically the same process.

Below centre
Peter McCaffrey waits for the scene to be set. The various dollies and mounts mean the camera can be used at a wide variety of heights above the ground.

Below right
Tools of the cameraman include a light meter, viewfinders and a colour chart. The colours on this chart have a known value so when filmed at the opening of a scene all other colours on the exposed film can be matched to it perfectly during post-production.

The actors' stand-ins walk through the scene so the cameras can check their angles and movements are working smoothly before the actors come onto the set. The scene is rehearsed several times, lights brought in and each frame of the shot perfected before the scene is filmed. When the scene includes a wide shot the camera operators work with the assistant directors to make sure the cast aren't being blocked by extras or props. If the camera operator sees that the bottom left of his frame is a bit empty, then some more flags or extras might be moved there to fill it in. Hours of work go in before the cameras start to record what may only take a moment to watch on the screen.

The first assistant cameraman works with the camera operator and adjusts the focus of the lens, which can change throughout the scene, especially when something is moving. A movie camera isn't like an ordinary camera, and doesn't have auto focus. Distances are measured out for a scene so that the actors know where to stand or where to move. The first assistant knows all the critical distances and can adjust the lens as the actor moves towards or away from the camera, which is called pulling the focus. A long measuring tape is used to check the distance from the actor to the camera.

The second assistant cameraman looks after all the equipment — the lenses and cameras — and has to get all the right equipment on set when it's needed on the set.

Space cam is a valuable tool for the DoP and involves a specialised camera attached to the body of a helicopter, which is used for aerial shots. Alfie Speight was the space cam helicopter pilot for *The Lion, the Witch and the Wardrobe* and flew space cam operator Steve Koster for the filming of crucial scenes. Each day before they took off they were given a list of shots — the places and things they needed to record, which sometimes includes what's called a plate shot. This is where the space cam shoots an empty scene and computer-generated characters are added later. To shoot an aerial shot of Aslan running and crossing a river they have to visualise him moving and then move the camera at the same height, speed and distance the lion would travel. Close-up computer-generated shots of him are then matched up with the outdoor film.

While they are in the air, Alfie concentrates on flying the helicopter safely and as smoothly and steadily as possible while Steve concentrates on the camera and a third person in the back checks that they're getting all the shots they need. For shooting plates, the pilot and camera operator have to imagine the scene — for example, Aslan sitting on a rock with the children on his back — and give him room to move and imagine which direction he is looking in.

Far left

DoP, Don McAlpine in front of his A camera team. He uses a light meter to check how much light there is in every scene, because the level of light changes all the time. Cloud can increase or decrease the available light by up to 20 per cent, which would affect the final result of the film.

Left

Even on a difficult terrain the camera must be completely level. The rock face seen here has been fabricated to create an elevated space for Peter's tent.

Below

The focus puller must first measure the distance between the lens and the subject that needs to be in focus. Because the camera operator can't tell what's in focus it is the focus puller's responsibility to make sure his timing and use of the focus mechanism is accurate. Here he looks at the screen and adjusts focus as the scene changes.

Tools of the trade

- *Light meter:* to measure the available light

- *Digital camera:* to record the colour saturation and light at the beginning of a scene as a reference if the scene has to be reshot later

- *Steadicam:* a special hand-held camera equipped with stabilisers that allow the cameraman to walk or run without their movement affecting the finished image — the film you see from this camera will travel smoothly without jumping up and down

- *Space cam:* a movie camera housed in a specially constructed sphere mounted on the front of a helicopter used for aerial filming, with stabilisers to compensate for any vibration from the helicopter. Because the space cam is very heavy, the helicopter needs to have a counter-balancing weight mounted on its tail boom.

blue screen, green screen

Using a green screen is a method of film making which allows the visual effects team to add computer-generated imagery (CGI) to film that has been shot on location with real actors. In *The Lion, the Witch and the Wardrobe* the head of the green screen department was David Thomson, and because the animals and fantasy creatures of Narnia speak and move and interact with human characters, green screen played a very important part. These screens can be either green or blue — for *The Lion, the Witch and the Wardrobe* they used green, other movies might use blue screens to achieve the same effect.

Green screens work because each colour in the spectrum has a different frequency, which gives it a unique 'temperature' that can be measured by a computer program. Green and blue don't blend in with other colours and are easy to distinguish, which makes them very easy to remove from the film. Once the green has been removed, the special effects team can add the computer-generated replacement image into the space it occupied. Green screen can be used to create a bigger army or crowd by filming 100 extras in front of a green screen, with computer-generated people added later to make the army look bigger.

It can also be used to add a background to a set. The coronation scene at Cair Paravel looks as if it was filmed on a clifftop, with views of the sea through the windows, but it was really filmed inside a studio. For these scenes, the space cam was used to film cliff faces and seascapes around the Catlins coast of New Zealand's South Island, which became the coast of Narnia on the big screen.

Centaurs at Cair Paravel. When the camera was shooting at low angles a wheeled horse section was added on the back to save CGI later. The front legs will still be added — hence the green screen trousers. They stand on a green box to give them extra height, and the boxes are also removed later.

The green screen department talk to the art department about the sets they are building and where each set will end, which determines where the green screens will be erected. When the DoP has worked out his camera moves, the green screen team can work out how big the screens will need to be, so they can be constructed out of special green cloth imported from Thailand. They are rigged to stand upright, and the team members have experience in rigging and scaffolding.

As well, the actors and extras who play creatures that are part human and part animal wear bright green tight-fitting clothing over the parts of their bodies that will be replaced with computer-generated animal bodies and legs. They have bright orange dots on them, called tracking marks, that act as reference points for the special effects so that when the computer-generated parts are added they move more naturally, with the right amount of weight displacement. All the actors playing fauns had to walk with their knees slightly bent because a goat's leg isn't straight like a human's, and if the actors walked upright their goat legs wouldn't look convincing. The tracking marks also help to keep everything in perspective, and are used to work out distances and depth of field, which affects what is in focus in the image.

The green screen department start work in the last three weeks of pre-production, and stay until the filming is completed. They work primarily with the art department and in this movie with wardrobe, as so many of the actors and extras needed to wear green screen clothing. Altogether there were seven in the team, working fulltime on *The Lion, the Witch and the Wardobe.*

Left
To achieve a view of London underneath the aircraft, a green screen was angled below the aeroplane. Notice the crane on an extended boom filming in the cockpit.

Below
Orange spots on the extras' trousers are used in post-production to add muscle movement.

Bottom left
Head of green screen, David Thomson (kneeling) adjusts his team's handiwork. Not just characters are given the green screen treatment. Any part of the background that needs to be replaced is also coated in the same green material.

clappers, gaffers, grips and best boys

The focus puller (standing in blue jeans) remotely adjusts the focus as the dolly grip tracks the camera along the rails for a low shot.

Above
Key grip Pat Nash (left) and gaffer Shaun Conway.

Above top
Grips need grunt. Sheer brute force is required to shift a 100 kW light up a steep bank at Aslan's Camp.

People reading movie credits are often mystified by strange titles such as clapper, grip, gaffer, best boy and get very confused when they hear about dolly grips! All of these are movie terms for various trades and essential people who work feverishly behind the scenes. Movies couldn't be made without them. For example, it can take these people anything up to three hours to set up a scene before filming can commence.

Pat Nash was the key grip on *The Lion, the Witch and the Wardrobe*, which made him head of the grips department. Grips are responsible for safety and movement of cameras — wherever the cameras have to go, they make sure it happens. They also look after all the hardware on site, such as camera cranes, dollies, tracks, and rigging. They have to work in every different physical situation where filming takes place — up mountains, in studios — and always make sure everything is secure and nothing flies away or falls off. They make sure everything is gripped — and that's how they get their name.

The key grip also supervises the riggers responsible for assembling the green screens. The riggers need to bolt together all the scaffolding that is needed for cameras, lights and screens. A grip's job is really about nuts and bolts and building everything the cameras need to operate, both in the studio and out on location — tracks for dollies, decks and frames and camera rigs to elevate the camera for a special shot.

Grips are also responsible for any cranes that have cameras mounted on them which can vary in size. The largest one used on *The Lion, the Witch and the Wardrobe* weighed 2.5 tonnes and was worth almost a million dollars. This means as well as operating it, they have to move it to wherever it is needed once it has been delivered to the set.

Each camera has its own grip and because they operate the dolly, or mobile mount for the camera (often on wheels but sometimes on a boom), not surprisingly they're called dolly grips. They stay with their camera and camera operator and make sure that if the camera has to move it moves at exactly the right time and to exactly the right place. It is a very difficult and responsible task. Often each camera move has to be repeated over and over in exactly the same way while the director and the DoP perfect the shot. Put simply, the camera operator moves himself and the camera, while the dolly grip pushes the dolly or operates a remote control if the camera is mounted on a boom. If the dolly grip doesn't get the camera to exactly the right place, even by a couple of centimetres, then the focus will be out and the image blurry. The key grip works closely with the director, the DoP and the camera operators. The grips and the camera operators all have connecting radio earpieces so they can communicate with each other quickly and efficiently as communication is vital.

The key grip begins working on the movie about six weeks before production starts and surveys the locations to see what sort of logistical problems there may be for his team. On this movie this meant locations in three different countries including places where equipment had to be set up in remote and inaccessible sites.

When the director and the DoP have decided to use a moving shot, and the camera needs to track, or move smoothly in and out or across the set, metal tracks are laid to transport the dolly. This requires lots of scaffolding and large trucks and containers to transport them.

Above left
Wooden wedges are an essential part of a grip's tools and used to level the track.

Above right
Patrick McArdle checks the gate.

Below left
The third member of the camera team is the clapper loader, and each camera has its own clapper loader. Their responsibilities are to load and change film, put the lenses in the camera, make sure they're clean and operate the clapperboard. Traditionally, this was a slate with a pair of hinged boards on top. Information such as the date, name of the film and number of scene and take is written on the slate and read aloud. The slate is filmed at the start of each take, when the boards were clapped together to provide a reference point for the editor to synchronise sound and film.

Below right
The modern clapper still records information about the scene, take, film roll and camera but now has a digital timer in the middle for accurate synchronisation of timing in post-production.

With all the heavy equipment on site and people working high above the ground, safety is a major consideration and anyone operating heavy equipment or building scaffolding to hold heavy equipment has to have the right trade qualifications.

Shaun Conway was the gaffer for *The Lion, the Witch and the Wardrobe* and is the chief lighting technician in charge of all lighting and electrical supply on the set. He needs to collaborate with the DoP or camera operators to come up with a style and feel for the lighting that suits the film. They need to think about whether it is a soft-lit film or a hard-lit film. A hard-lit film would be something set in the desert where there is a lot of hard sunlight. A soft-lit film would be set in somewhere like Europe where there is a lot of atmosphere in the air. There are also other things to consider — is it a fantasy or is it real life? The lighting should suit the film in that way.

The best boy is the number one electrician in charge of a group of boys. On *The Lion, the Witch and the Wardrobe* Shaun had 30 lighting crew, and the best boy was Moses Fotofili. As Shaun said: 'they are the boys and he is the best. As simple as that. These names have been around for many years — gaffer is an old English name for a foreman.'

Sets have to be lit differently for each scene and the set needs to be ready and prepared before shooting starts so the director can move around and pick his shots without waiting too long. Even scenes taken outside in brilliant sunshine need lighting, and screens to bounce light onto the set at the right angle to achieve the effect the director and DoP are looking for. For *The Lion, the Witch and the Wardrobe* this meant setting up electrical supplies in some very remote places, using generators and 25 kilometres of electrical cable.

When filming takes place outside the studio, the gaffer's concern is about light control more than anything. The sun can be either a help or a hindrance. You are controlling the sun — working with it or cutting it out completely if it's coming from the wrong direction. Over a day it goes from one side of a set to the other, and even if the team is putting a scene together that only lasts a minute on screen you have to maintain lighting continuity. You can't change it around in a way that it doesn't change in real life.

In the studio you can do whatever you want and you put the lights in where the sun should be and leave them there. Big screens are used to soften the light as making a smaller light source bigger also means you can make it softer. A small light source is hard and a large one is soft. When lighting the actors' faces, it is more complimentary to use a soft light.

If you think about the sky as one big soft light, then that is what the lighting team is trying to match. What they do is to take what nature provides and emulate or amplify it, putting light where it needs to be for the camera which then puts it on the big screen.

The amazing ice sets on *The Lion, the Witch and the Wardrobe* were a challenge for the lighting crew, who had never worked on anything like this before. Because the ice was transparent they had to light the set through the ice, producing a brilliantly magical effect.

Opposite above
Shaun Conway radios information to another member of the lighting crew. A diffuser and screen are in the background.

Opposite below
Screens can also be placed over an actor's head to reduce the sun's glare.

Above left
Dean Wright holds Aslan's head before using it as a reference point for the actors. A real lion might have meant hiring twice as many actors!

Above centre
Despite bright sunshine, powerful lights are still needed to remove shadows and create even luminance on the actor's face.

Above right
Here a screen is being used to soften the light. Rather than pointing it directly at the actors, the soft light reflected back from the screen creates a natural light.

Lighting equipment for The Lion, the Witch and the Wardrobe

- Lights including 100 kilowatt lamps
- 50 kilowatt lamps
- Portable generators
- Electrical cable
- Lighting screens

Some of the animals of Narnia wait in line at Aslan's Camp, filmed near Oamaru.

Sled Reynolds with Peter and his beautiful white unicorn.

the animals and creatures *of Narnia*

The world of Narnia is populated by many different animal and mythical beasts, some of which are part human, so the director had to use a combination of real and computer-generated creatures.

The animal supervisor for *The Lion, the Witch and the Wardrobe* was Sled Reynolds, and his team had to work with the real thing — mice, dogs, wolves and horses.

Much of the animal training, especially with the wolves, involved using food as an incentive. Basically they have to work for their food, and while they are very intelligent they aren't easy to work with as they can't be forced to do anything they don't want to.

Because New Zealand doesn't have wolves and is rabies free, they were imported from Los Angeles and had to spend time in quarantine before filming started. Ten wolves were used in *The Lion, the Witch and the Wardrobe*, seven males and three females. The wolves who play the key characters of Maugrim and Vardan are two-year-old brothers, called Ricky and Bob.

Because wolves are shy by nature their trainer, Timothy Williams, introduced them to a father figure when they were only three weeks old, a boxer called Champ, who now keeps them under control. He has a very placid nature, and because the wolves have known him since they were pups he is still the 'boss dog' even though he is now much smaller than them. He is used to keep them reassured and confident on a new set — he visits the set with the wolves and because he stays calm and relaxed, so do they. If the wolves start fighting amongst themselves, he is the one who can stop them.

Some of the horses on *The Lion, the Witch and the Wardrobe* had to play unicorns, and specially fitted horns were made which they had to get used to wearing. When Peter's unicorn had to rear up a trainer standing in front of the horse, but out of the camera shot, used a pair of lungeing whips to silently signal to the horse.

The creatures of Narnia were made to look real in different ways. One was by adding computer-generated animal limbs and bodies to human actors, another was through the use of prosthetics, make-up and costume. Some, like Aslan and the Beavers, were completely computer-generated while animatronics created the robotic reindeer that drew the Witch's sleigh.

Howard Berger was supervisor of special make-up, prosthetics and animatronics and looked after all the creatures. Special make-up effects is a little bit of everything. You have to know how to paint, sculpt, be a make-up artist, hairdresser, prop builder and costume rigger. *The Lion, the Witch and the Wardrobe* provided many challenges, and was one of the hardest films Howard had worked on. The make-up for each creature was very specific and because it's a movie for children there was no blood or gore or slime, which special make-up effects often have to provide. They play an important part in bringing to life fantasy characters the whole world already knows – but Howard particularly wanted to be faithful to Andrew Adamson's childhood memories of the book.

Above
Boxer 'Champ' with one of his 'children'. The wolves were only allowed on closed sets and housed in specially controlled areas due to New Zealand's very strict animal and quarantine rules.

Below
A wolf on set. Note the small bag he has his front paws on — the wolves are trained to stand on this while waiting for a command during filming.

Above
A load of faun dummies have their hair and make-up added by Weta staff.

Below left
Howard Berger applies contact lenses to a satyr during the make-up process.

Below right
Close-up shots of animals with full head and body prosthetics were used for foregrounds shots with animated figures filling the background. This procedure allowed a small number of extras to be multiplied into thousands.

Characters like Mr Tumnus had prosthetic faun ears that had to look convincing, and prosthetic body suits were used for the witches, ogres, boggles and cyclops. These were made from latex to fit the extras. Whole heads had to be made for creatures like the Minotaurs and they used a lot of fake fur. Howard and his team were kept constantly busy applying make-up and prosthetics, often starting at 3.30 in the morning to have them all ready for shooting at 9.00 a.m. Their record was 83 different prosthetic creatures in one day.

As well as working on such a large scale, very small but important details are also necessary — for example, the White Witch's eyes change colour in the stone table scene and Howard needed to organise coloured contact lenses and special make-up to dye her lashes red.

Above right
Extras walk down through the rocks at Flock Hill after arriving by helicopter.

Above left, left and below
The work of many people behind the scenes created an amazing menagerie of animals and creatures from Narnia — a magical world where animals talk and interact with humans.

making
trees *and* gardens

Above
Silk flowers adorn the springtime garden in Narnia. Although made of silk they look very realistic, even at close range.

Right above
On the set most of the trees were attached to steel rods concreted into the ground. A slot was cut up the back of the tree, and the tree lowered into position using a crane, then bolted to the steel. A team of plasterers and scenic artists covered over all the bolts and steel.

Right below
For springtime in Narnia two sets were decorated, one with a scattering of flowers showing early spring and the other with 600 plants, some real and some made of silk. Russell Hoffman and his team spent weeks dressing the main set to make the plantings look realistic.

The greens department is part of the art department and put together all the green material for the sets — all the plants, trees, forests and any gardens. Head of the greens department for *The Lion, the Witch and the Wardrobe* was Russell Hoffman, who worked with a team of 21 greensmen.

Part of his brief was to recreate a Northern European forest in New Zealand that would match scenes to be shot in the Czech Republic. He started by researching tree species available in New Zealand that would also be found in Europe. Because New Zealand has a temperate climate there were several exotic species that were perfect — including European larch and Douglas fir.

The art directors put together a tree plot and Russell's team visited forests with an arborist to find suitable trees for the Lantern Waste, to be transported back to the studio. This could take four to five days so they needed to plan well in advance of the shooting schedule. The tallest trees used in Lantern Waste were 11 metres tall and wooden cradles held the branches off the deck of the truck.

The location of the great battle was sown with special grasses in the autumn before filming took place so that they would have time to grow thick and lush. This was needed because the location was in the South Island high country, where these types of grasses wouldn't normally grow. The whole area was watered using helicopters and monsoon buckets.

Two catering companies were used to feed the cast and crew during filming, Bonifant and Saxby in the North Island and Flying Trestles in the South. The South Island catering supervisor was Sue Henry. The caterers need to feed everyone on set and it's important not to run out of food. Organising daily deliveries of fresh food for up to 500 people at a time kept Sue busy. Menus had to be planned that took into account the weather and the sort of food people wanted — with most meals catered for on a self-serve buffet system, in a huge catering marquee capable of seating 600 people at a time.

Sometimes catering had to provide hot boxes when crew couldn't leave the site to come to the catering tent, and hot drinks and freshly baked snacks were always available during shooting.

All the food was cooked fresh each day on site, and when there is no corner dairy for another kilo of bacon, the caterers need plenty of back-up supplies. A first priority is working out supply lines for the daily delivery of fresh ingredients.

In the South Island there were 16 caterers split into crews working different shifts, as day and night shoots mean people need to be fed at all hours. A typical day for Sue would start at 3.00 a.m. going through to about 4.30 p.m., with another crew starting in the afternoon and working until 11.00 p.m. When people are working hard they need lots of healthy, tasty food. As Sue describes it, 'We try to make people happy — if they are, we are. We've done our job.'

feeding
the troops

Above
Generally menus are planned seven days ahead and rotated so they might have a spicy day then a plain day, using beef, pork, chicken or fish, trying not to have any of these two days in a row.

Left above
Fresh ingredients are used at all times to provide an interesting and varied diet.

Left below
The huge marquee for feeding the troops. The efficiency of the catering staff fed over 600 people three courses in less than an hour.

on the set

Below

The stone table set was filmed in a small studio at Hobsonville. Whenever live flames are used a number of safety officers stand by to light and extinguish the torches, as any small mistake would have disastrous results.

Opposite above

Robert Moxham checks a scene prior to shooting. It is his responsibility to ensure the filmed scene has all the props in the right places.

Opposite below

Silence on set is a necessity. No cellphones, no coughing. Lights are strategically placed around the entire area and if the light is flashing — don't make a sound!

A movie set is a hive of activity, with lots of different departments working at the same time, each with their own priorities. Someone needs to control all the traffic and keep things on schedule and the person who does this is the Assistant Director, or AD. The AD for *The Lion, the Witch and the Wardrobe* was KC Hodenfield, who manages all of this with the help of the second and third ADs.

KC started by scouting locations in Europe, long before shooting started, and began fulltime preparations by drawing up a schedule based on the script and how long he estimated filming was going to take, based on his experience. With 240 scenes to be shot, he estimated around 100-150 days. This schedule became the database of what had to go in each scene — props, weapons, greenery, extras. The schedule went to each department so they all knew what they needed to have ready and by when, scene by scene.

As well as assisting the director, the AD is also responsible for safety on set. While the director deals with the actors the AD's function is to make sure everybody knows what they should be doing right now, tomorrow and the next day. Sometimes the AD has to yell at people if they're doing something foolish, so having a loud voice comes in very handy, especially in wide open spaces.

In *The Lion, the Witch and the Wardrobe* KC was dealing with 75 extras in Aslan's army, which with special effects became 5000, with 80 more in the Witch's army becoming 10,000 in the finished movie.

Filming is ready to go when the AD has everyone in a particular scene on set and in place, and all the technical crews have completed their tasks. He then closes the set and calls for quiet and then for cameras to start rolling and sound to start recording before the director calls action and the shot begins. The call for action and cameras rolling is repeated all over the set and surrounding area so everyone knows to keep quiet and keep out of shot.

The set decorator, Kerry Brown, was in charge of dressing the sets with all the right props before the film crew arrived. Her job also started a long time before filming, and meant buying or designing all of the items that would be needed to dress each scene. Many are made especially and others are sourced — props people may have to travel to other countries to find exactly the right prop for an important scene. Kerry then worked ahead of time dressing the sets before the shooting crew arrived each day, and packing it all up again when they left.

Opposite
The tremendous attention to detail on set. These items are a long way from the action but they pass even the closest inspection.

Above
The Witch's chariot was motorised so she could be filmed in motion for the battle scene, with the polar bears added later.

Above top left

The AD has a huge job on set — they are the main line of communication between the director and all the crew and extras.

Above top right

KC and Andrew check a scene at Flock Hill. These two people have a very close working relationship — both able to work calmly and fully focussed despite the pressure of a huge number of people.

Above

KC and 2nd AD Jeff Okabayashi prepare to film the coronation at Cair Paravel.

This meant researching the historical period for the wartime scenes and liaising with the art department. For Aslan's Camp, her team had to design and make 75 silk medieval-style tents and all the camp dressings. A team of 17 people worked for five months just to put the designs onto the tents in gold leaf.

Another important person on the set is the on set art director, also known as the on set standby props. Their job is to make sure everything the art department has made and anything that's in front of camera — every cup of coffee, animal, car, horse or chair — looks perfect and fits in with the period or whatever is appropriate to the shot.

There is no room for mistakes — if the standby props gets something wrong the scene has to be shot again, costing valuable time as well as money. The standby props for *The Lion, the Witch and the Wardrobe* was Robert Moxham, or Moxie.

Props for a movie come from everywhere. Moxie went through the script and did a breakdown with the propmaster, and set dresser, who were in charge of getting all the props and set dressings together. His main job is at the end of the chain when all the props have been assembled and the look for the movie is finalised. Then he works with director and camera operator, who is the one with his eye through the lens all the time and who sometimes needs him to rearrange things for a better shot.

As well as the director and camera operator, the third person Moxie works with is the AD who is controlling the set and will want to know: Is that set ready? Are you ready to film? Is it looking good?

Before the cameras start to roll, the set has to be perfect — so Moxie had an on set dresser to look after all the furnishings, make sure the cushions are fluffed, the curtains are straight, the windows are clean and the carpet has been vacuumed. He also had a painter, a carpenter and sometimes a plasterer. If the set is outside there were up to 20 people helping him, as well as the greens crew, each with a specific job, and everyone fitting together like cogs in a wheel to make sure everything runs smoothly.

All the physical effects that move in real time on the set are the responsibility of the Head of Physical and Mechanical Special Effects. For *The Lion, the Witch and the Wardrobe* this was Jason Durey, who was in control of all the smoke, snow, wind, mechanical rigs like the Witch's sleigh with its robotic reindeer, her chariot, the Heinkel He-111 bomber and all the fires in the movie.

There were 46 working in Jason's team, all with a multitude of skills but also specialist electricians and fitters and turners, using every kind of tool, from mills, lathes, presses, cutting saws, carpentry gear, band saws, rock-breaking tools, flame throwers, hydraulic power packs and specialised gas equipment.

Above
Patrick McArdle operating the focussing mechanism for A camera. The camera is over 300 metres from his position.

Below
The 'dummy' Aslan was used on set to ensure accurate placing of the CGI Aslan later. Moxie and William prepare for shooting while the focus length is checked.

recording
the sounds of Narnia

Above
Filming a piece for a Disney promotional advertisement. The sound this time is picked up by a smaller boom mike. The 'fluffy' cover helps reduce wind noise through the mike.

Below
A boom mike used for recording the live sound. The weighty boom has to be held steady for minutes on end at a height so it isn't seen in the film. The sound is then recorded digitally.

The production sound mixer for *The Lion, the Witch and the Wardrobe* was Tony Johnson, who records all the sound that happens on the day in front of the cameras. He also mixes the background and foreground sound together in the way that will work best for that scene. Some of these sounds will make it into the final movie, some may be removed in the sound editing that happens later. Some other sounds may be added or enhanced if they haven't been captured effectively on set.

For example if there are a lot of planes or background noises they need to be removed and more appropriate sound added in. The main priority for the sound recorder is capturing all the dialogue — the words spoken by the actors.

Emotional scenes can be difficult for any actor. Andrew didn't want the children to have to do these scenes over and over, because repeating that sort of performance is very difficult, especially for young actors who don't have as much experience as the rest of the cast. Tony's most important contribution to the film was to get their best performances recorded for him, because sometimes what you film on the day can never be repeated or captured again.

The sound for *The Lion, the Witch and the Wardrobe* was recorded on a computer, and every time Tony recorded some sound it made its own file. While filming was taking place, Tony could be hearing sound from several different microphones at once. This meant there was a lot more control in the post-production sound department where they fine-tuned all of his sound recordings. They were able to exercise a lot of control over it because the computer could separate all the sound into different components. Because computers can sometimes crash, Tony always worked with two machines, using one as a backup.

As well as background sound the sound recorder also has to deal with unwanted sound coming from all the other things happening on the set such as noisy lighting gear, cameras and all the equipment they use, cranes, the people on set, special effects, wind — everything creating noise.

Recording the sound is different on every movie. *The Lion, the Witch and the Wardrobe* has a lot of dialogue with lots of scenes where the actors are talking in conditions that were very noisy, especially for the great battle. Tony used a lot of radio mikes to try and keep background noises down. These are small portable microphones hidden in the actors' costumes, which transmit the sound by radio so the sound recorder doesn't need to rely on the boom mike. Fortunately the costume department was able to find places in the actors' clothing that worked brilliantly.

Above
Sometimes sound is recorded from different microphones. Here a mike is hidden in Oreius' uniform. His sounds are recorded on one channel while a boom mike is used to pick up the sound of Edmund.

Below
Tony at his mobile recording studio. He normally places the unit in a quiet place where he can hear the sound uninterrupted so he can report back immediately if the recording is satisfactory.

let it snow!

Above
Part of the set at Kelly Park. These drifts of snow are made from shredded paper. Many of the film makers wore dust masks as the fake snow created a lot of dust. The author's camera needed a 30-minute clean every night to remove the tiny particles.

Below left
Peter Cleveland at work. He is an experienced skier who loves hitting the real slopes as much as creating them.

Below right
The snow at Paradise was a different type to that created inside at Kelly Park. A special synthetic material was mixed with water to create instant snow. Once used it was vacuumed up to return the site to its original condition.

When the children visit Narnia they find a frozen land that has been locked into a thousand years of winter by the White Witch. Scenes with heavy snow were filmed in the Czech Republic, but for the scenes filmed in New Zealand and in the studio, the set decorators needed realistic-looking snow that wouldn't melt under the hot lights, or get sludgy and dirty when the actors and extras walked over it again and again during filming.

Peter Cleveland was appointed snow chief, and he needed to create huge amounts of artificial snow to cover the sets for the early scenes, and smaller drifts of melting snow for the springtime scenes showing Narnia slowly waking after the Witch's winter is defeated.

There were seven different materials used to make snow in Narnia — from shredded paper and the insides of disposable nappies or diapers, which are chopped up and sprayed around by huge guns, to a water-based apoxin. When water and air are mixed with it, 'snowflakes' form. The ceiling in the studio was plumbed so that Peter could make it snow gently over the entire set. After each take the snow had to be resprayed to cover the tracks made by people and animals. Because making snow can be very dusty, all the snow makers needed to wear masks while they were working, and from time to time massive extractor fans were used to suck the dust out of the air.

After years of preparation and planning the land of Narnia was ready for the cameras. The actors had learned their lines, been costumed and made up, but now they had to become the children, the Witch, the Professor, Mr Tumnus, Oreius, General Otmin and all the other characters.

Andrew Adamson knew exactly how he wanted each character to react in each scene. He wanted to capture a sense of wonder when Georgie Henley (Lucy) first sees James McAvoy (Mr Tumnus) so she was never shown what he would look like. She was led onto the Lantern Waste set blindfolded and the blindfold removed as she stood in front of him, with the cameras rolling to capture her genuine surprise.

Tilda Swinton had the difficult task of making her character credible to all those who had read the book and had their own idea of what the White Witch would be like. At the same time she had to appear with much less make-up than she was used to — something she found quite different. As a mother herself she was particularly moved by the scene where the children are sent away to stay with the Professor.

Part of the challenge for the actors was that many of the characters being CGI, they often had to act very emotional scenes with a character that wasn't there, just using their imagination.

To tell the story in movie form Andrew and the screenwriter needed to expand the secondary characters and even name some, like Ginnarbrik. Sometimes they created new ones. Shane Rangi played the Minotaur General Otmin — while his character isn't in the book, every queen has to have an army and every army has to have a general.

As a Minotaur, Shane had to work inside a huge animatronic head. He couldn't see anything when he was wearing it and had to trust that the people guiding him onto the set were putting him into the right place to hit his marks for the camera. For the scene where he walks down from the stone table after the White Witch kills Aslan, he had to try hard not to think about falling. It was very hot and claustrophobic inside the heavy head and in two and a half weeks of filming he lost 14 kg.

bringing the **characters** *to life*

Bottom left
The character of Mr Tumnus was a critical test for the audience — the first part-CGI character the audience sees.

Bottom right
Shane Rangi without his Minotaur head.

Below
Patrick Kake with his heavy hero sword.

Actors whose characters needed prosthetics and creature make-up, like Patrick Kake, who played Aslan's chief centaur, Oreius, needed to be in the make-up chair by 3.15 a.m., having his prosthetics glued on and hair attached to his back. Having his make-up done, wig arranged and getting into his costume could take up to four hours.

Oreius needed to be a strong, muscular, silent type of character, letting his physical presence do the talking. He also needed to be skilful with a sword and strong enough to wield two heavy hero swords at a time. When his character was fighting hand to hand with another actor or stuntman, Patrick needed to be careful not to hurt them as the weapons were capable of causing serious injury. He kept his strength up during filming by exercising every day — running 5 km, doing 100 press-ups and around 120 crunches and leg lifts and training 4–5 times a week at the gym.

Above left
It takes a lot of skill to be able to perform as if you are a normal person when you are walking around with a bull's head on your shoulders. You have to look as if you know where you're going, with strong confident body movements that are true to the character so the team operating the animatronic head can match the movement of the face to the actor's body. The mouth on the head is moved by remote control. Four different people made General Otmin — a human actor in a suit with an animatronic head operated by remote control, with digital legs added on by someone in the visual FX team and a different actor providing his voice.

Above right
Andrew and Tilda share ideas about the scene at Aslan's Camp.

Right
The actors playing the children had demanding roles, each with a very different character and emotional journey.

While the camera and lighting teams are setting up a shot, they need the actors in place, but this would mean hours of standing around which would make it very hard for them to give a good performance when it was needed. To get around this, stand-ins, who match the physical attributes of each lead actor, are used instead. Photo doubles are used to film shots where the character's face isn't seen so the real actor can be filming another scene somewhere else at the same time.

Dana Porter was Tilda Swinton's stunt double, and also did stuntwork as a female centaur. She is experienced in horse riding, gymnastics, diving, rock-climbing and martial arts. Her role included a lot of sword fighting, which was choreographed for her to rehearse before it was taught to Tilda. Dana worked with both Tilda and William and also did a lot of training with Skandar as well, all working hard to make sure the sword fights looked real in front of the camera.

Extras are used for non-speaking roles, or for roles that may only say a few words, for example, in a crowd scene. They are the people who populate a movie, and are there in the background behind the main actors. In *The Lion, the Witch and the Wardrobe* they were used mainly in the big spectacular scenes, for the stone table, the battle and at Cair Paravel.

stand-ins, photo doubles, stuntmen *and* extras

Above and left
Extras spend a lot of time waiting for their five minutes of fame. A drink and a good book help pass the time for some, while others can sit in the sun and watch the action. The suits were so big and cumbersome that for many, between takes was a time to lie down and rest.

Top

Dana Porter: 'For the camera it looks as if you're hitting them really hard. You learn to strike and stop. When you're training with actors who don't pull up you have to learn to block or you're going to get hit. It's different working with a stuntie, then we hardly touch whereas with actors we have to block.'

Centre

Seven helicopters worked for over an hour to transport cast and crew and all their equipment to the 'helicopter only' set at Flock Hill.

Bottom left

Josh Leys was both the stand-in and photo double for William Moseley (Peter), and described his role: 'They use me instead of the actor because being an actor you have to focus on your acting — you don't need to know the technical stuff. We do that for them so they can give their best performance.'

Bottom centre

A lot of time is spent standing in place while the crew prepare the shot. Between each take water is supplied but once the decision is made to remove heads and stand down, the AD knows it will take at least 30 minutes to get all the heads back on and the extras back on set.

Bottom right

Three of the stand-ins and photo doubles on set at Paradise. Left to right: Felicity Hamill (Lucy), Josh Leys (Peter) and Charlotte Hayes (Susan).

lonely landscapes

Two places that appear in the movie weren't even visited by the cast. The sea coast of the Catlins District (above) in the south-east of the South Island was used as the landscape for Cair Paravel, and transplanted to the scene using the magic of CGI. The dramatic sea cliffs and pounding waves were a three-dimensional reproduction of the words of CS Lewis.

The Severn Valley Railway near Ludlow in Shropshire (below left) was the ideal location to film the children's journey to the Professor's house. Original operating steam trains and period stations provided authentic scenes of Britain's wartime railway, which was then used to recreate the children's arrival in the country.

The steep, inaccessible area of Flock Hill and its amazingly shaped rocks (below right) were used for filming part of the great battle scene, but normally they are lonely and remote.

computer
wizardry

The ingenuity of a number of people created a way for Oreius to appear as if he was running. First place the actor with green screen trousers on the back of a truck at the same height above the ground as a horse. Then mount the 2nd Unit camera on the front of the truck and drive it down the area known as 'Chariot Run' at the same speed a horse would gallop. The result in the film is a smooth integration of reality and special effects.

Motion-capture (MoCap) cameras placed on set do exactly that — capture the motion so it can be analysed and used on the post-production CGI process.

Special effects are illusions movie makers use to create scenes that would be difficult or even impossible to film in the real world, and are used to serve the dramatic interests of the story the director wants to tell.

There are two kinds of special effects — visual and photographic, which manipulate the film or image, and mechanical or physical effects. *The Lion, the Witch and the Wardrobe* relied heavily on visual effects to portray the fantasy elements needed to create Narnia and its creatures, and the visual effects (VFX) supervisor was Dean Wright. His responsibility was to oversee the design, planning, execution and final delivery of all the visual effects Andrew needed to enrich the story, and his team worked with specialist VFX companies, one of which was Rhythm and Hues.

Dean had to interpret what Andrew wanted to achieve with each scene and then brief the people working on the special effects so that all the digital supervisors, artists and animators could create the shots. Part of his job was to make sure everyone was keeping to the schedule as well as keeping an eye on the overall quality control of all the VFX. In *The Lion, the Witch and the Wardrobe* VFX was used to create full hero characters like Aslan and the Beavers, as well as up to sixty different types of animated creatures and their environments. It was important to make sure that the CGI characters didn't come across as cartoon characters; they had to look like living, breathing, feeling, intelligent animals capable of expressing deep emotions so audiences would accept and believe in them.

Computer animation is a technique in which an image stored on a computer is moved by digital manipulation. The animator specifies the key position of the moving object in each frame and the computer program fills in all the movements in between.

Computer-generated imagery (CGI) creates animated images in a computer which can be digitally combined with live action. It can be used for characters or other elements such as scenery or weather.

Matte painting is a technique where a painting or object is combined with other elements in a camera shot and used to fill an unexposed area on the film left when live actors were filmed by a camera partially covered by a matte.

A matte covers part of a camera lens keeping that part of the film unexposed so a different element can be added later.

Left above
Dean Wright with Aslan. Dean used the full-sized Aslan as a place holder before he was replaced with the computer-generated version in post-production.

Left
A model of the chariot pulled by polar bears made by the art department.

Below left
The space cam mounted on the nose of the Heliworks Squirrel. Quite often a set take will start close to the ground with a boom shot and then recede rapidly, with the space cam shot (and CGI) taking over.

Below right
Prosthetic heads were used in the film when close-up shots were required which are very difficult to do with CGI.

voices
in the dark

Movies with animated characters need actors to provide the voices the audience hear in the final movie. They need to be able to 'act' with their voices as they can't show emotions by using body language or facial expressions — they have to do it all with the tone of their voice.

In *The Lion, the Witch and the Wardrobe* animal characters like the wolves and CGI characters who speak, such as Aslan, the Fox and the Beavers, had their voices recorded by actors working thousands of kilometres away on the other side of the world.

Because the story was written by an English author, the children and all the animals needed to speak with English accents. Mr and Mrs Beaver were played by Ray Winstone and Dawn French, and the Fox was played by Rupert Everett. Their voices were recorded in a sound studio in England and added to the film in the final editing.

The actors had to watch how their characters appeared in each scene so they could match their timing and voice tone to what was happening on the screen. If their character looked startled then their voice needed to sound startled. If their character had been running or was exhausted, they also had to make their voice match the character's physical movements.

All the speaking characters with animatronic heads had to have their voices added later as well, with the actors' voices synchronised to match the movement of the mouth pieces in the heads, which were operated on set by remote control.

Leading English actor Dawn French provided the voice for Mrs Beaver. While she visited the location in New Zealand, and met the actors playing the children, her lines of dialogue were recorded in England and then put together with the voices of the other actors. Some of these were recorded in England, in a sound studio, and some in New Zealand, during filming. All of these were combined in the sound editing.

mixing the *sound*

mixing the
sound

The voice of Father Christmas was mixed with the voices of the other children in post-production to ensure all the sounds had a moderated volume level.

When you go to the movies, you hear a mix of dialogue, sound effects and music. While you hear all three at the same time, they are recorded separately and combined by sound editors. All the dialogue and sounds recorded on the set will appear on a production track, the music for the score will be recorded separately and sound effects that weren't recorded on set can be created after filming finishes, in post-production.

Sound editors work with the director and editor to fix any problem with the sound recorded on the set, sometimes adding extra sounds or rerecording dialogue. This is done in a 'looping session', where actors redo dialogue that might not have recorded clearly or which the director needs to change to match the way he's cutting the final movie. While libraries of prerecorded sounds are sometimes used for special sounds, Aslan's roar and the White Witch's wand sound were created by sound designer Richard Beggs. Computerised sound effects consoles let the sound editors manipulate and clean up both created and recorded sounds.

The final sound mix is sometimes called dubbing, and is carried out by the mixer, who can blend together as many as 15 different sound track elements, making sure that each sound has the right emphasis. The mixer also has to make decisions about which channel each sound should be heard in, to achieve a realistic stereo effect. Once the mix is finished, it is recorded on a digital sound track which stores the sound information directly on the film, or on compact discs that play in sync with the projector.

Sound mixing terms

- *Foley artist:* a person who creates sound effects like glass breaking, someone falling to the ground or the sound of distant thunder, that either happen out of view or were not recorded during filming

- *Background noise:* any noise or sound happening in the background of a scene which is used to make that scene more realistic — the murmur of waves or people talking in another room

- *Balance:* making sure that no one sound dominates when it shouldn't — keeping all the different sounds in a scene relative to one another to match reality

- *Digital sound track:* records sound in a digital form that can be stored in a computer

- *Dolby:* a trademarked stereo and noise-reduction system to generate up to seven channel sound

- *DTS:* Digital theatre sound

- *Postsync:* recording sounds in post-production after filming has finished, which will be synchronised with the filmed images in the final movie

editing
and
continuity

The essential tools for editing include a computer with a powerful hard drive able to store a huge quantity of data, a tape deck to transfer film to video, digitising hardware and editing software. Sim Evan-Jones uses three monitors, two for data and one large monitor to carry out a highly sophisticated cut and paste.

Once a scene has been filmed there is a huge amount of footage, with shots (takes) from different angles, or different versions the director has tried — some good, some not so good — which the editors cut and paste together. The editors are the final filter, distilling everyone's efforts to best tell the story. The head of editing for *The Lion, the Witch and the Wardrobe* was Sim Evan-Jones, who worked with second editor Jim May and a team of editing assistants.

The editors worked in two distinct stages — working on footage to give to the VFX teams to add in the CGI characters, and then bringing everything together at the end once they had been added. When they started the first stage, 20 per cent of the characters didn't exist, so they used temporary visual effects for the CGIs — little computerised stand-ins.

The editors had to work quickly, and for long hours. If film was shot Tuesday, by Wednesday they needed to have added in the audio elements and cut the scene together for Andrew to comment on before they began to refine it. They constantly referred back to the pre-vis computer mock-up so they knew what to expect and how all the scenes needed to fit together.

All the tapes they used were digitised and stored on a huge server, and the two editors shared the cutting. They needed to keep up with filming so that everything was cut soon after they finished shooting, then they spent over a year refining the editing, with three months to add special effects before the movie score was put in near the end.

When they were cutting they needed to check that they hadn't missed anything important. If they ended up with no close-ups of Lucy, they had to find some to cut in, or they might have too much of the Beavers or a battle scene going on for too long. Often they cut 20 versions of a scene before they were satisfied.

The editors needed a good understanding of what Andrew was looking for, his sense of comic timing and what sort of character arcs he was after. A character shouldn't start and end their story without having changed in some way. Something has to happen to them over the course of the story, and they have to go through what is called an arc, something which challenges them and takes them from A to B. Several of the characters in *The Lion, the Witch and the Wardrobe* go though a mythic journey and the film needed to be cut to show this.

The blitz scene at the opening of the film was a new piece written specifically for the film. Tight editing creates a sense of urgency that explains for modern audiences why the children needed to leave London for the relative safety of the countryside. This explanation would have been unnecessary for readers when the book was first written.

Because the director can't look at every piece of footage, the editors have to do that for him and make decisions on which pieces to include and which to leave out. A great editor, Walter Murch, once explained his job to a little girl who said, 'Well you just take out the bad bits.' Ultimately that is what editors are there to do — take out everything that doesn't help the story.

Because the actors had to imagine the CGI characters, this impacted on the editing. In the scenes with Aslan they had to pretend he was there even though it might have been his model stand-in or someone in a lion suit. The editing had to give the lion character, and the actors needed to be shown responding emotionally to him. Aslan had to have a great heart, the Beavers had to be funny and the editors had to direct the effects people on how to achieve this.

Script supervisor Alexa Alden had the vital task of keeping a record of every shot in the movie, to make sure continuity was maintained. Sometimes called a take sheet, her notes recorded the number and duration of each shot, where the actors were, which direction they moved in and what dialogue was spoken. Continuity is very important in movies, which are often shot out of sequence. The finished movie must have a logical transition from scene to scene and shot to shot, with everything matched meticulously so that the finished movie 'happens' in real time and doesn't jump about with objects or marks on actors' faces appearing and disappearing, which is what happens if the continuity isn't done properly. It is a highly skilled and very significant role, and the editors depend on the script supervisor so that when they are cutting and pasting scenes or takes together everything flows smoothly.

Above
Alexa Alden has to concentrate on set at all times to make sure continuity is maintained between each scene. This important information might also be used to maintain continuity if later pick-ups are required.

Below
Jim May at work. The editorial team have to have an intimate knowledge of film making and their director. They can then work on the raw material and produce elements edited together in a style the director wants.

adding the
special
effects

Dean Wright holds the model Beavers up for placement filming. The models were shot with the actors and later replaced by computer-generated versions of the Beavers. The complex nature of the CGI meant that once a scene was shot with real people, it had to be shot again several times to capture all the items needed later.

Because almost every scene in the movie has some element of computer-generated special effects, filming a scene doesn't finish when the director calls 'Check the gate'. Everyone clears the set and the cameras film a clean plate, which is the set filmed using the same camera movements without any actors in place. This is for the visual effects team, so that they can place and move the CGI characters in that scene and have them interact naturally with the live actors. If necessary they can even move the actors around so the movie the audience sees is a seamless blending of real and CGI characters.

While each scene is being filmed with the actors and extras, another team is shooting for motion capture, or MoCap. Small digital video cameras around the set capture the movement of all the green screen parts of the characters — like the fauns' legs. These cameras are set up on tall tripods to record the characters' physical movements from different angles. This helps make the final CGI part of the movie look realistic and three dimensional.

A process called High Dynamic Range Radiance Imaging (HDRI) uses six cameras with fish-eye lenses to take a snapshot of the lighting and the position and strength of the sun, recording the range of light from the light to dark in every scene. This information is also necessary for the visual effects department. The camera operators film two spheres, or balls, on the empty set. A shiny chrome ball reflects almost a 360-degree map of the set. The information from this helps the CGI team to light their computer-generated character so that the light falls on them exactly as it would have done if they were there.

A theodolite captured the exact shape of the physical location for each scene. This data helped to perfectly blend the computer-generated elements into the final shot.

Because colours look different as the light changes, a second ball is filmed in the same way to provide a grey scale level, information used to match the colour of the CGI character to the lighting conditions at the time.

For complex CGI characters like the Beavers, stuffed life-size stand-ins are put into the set to record the light and shade that would have fallen on them at the time the scene was filmed. If light hits a character in a particular way as they move through a scene the visual effects team need to know so they can show that in the final movie.

HDRI technology allows the CGI team to create a virtual set in the computer so that as they build the characters, light comes at them from the right direction as they move and interact with the live actors, all of which helps make them look real and convincing. This work is highly skilled and specialised and takes a long time, using powerful computer programs developed for movie animation. Because so much of *The Lion, the Witch and the Wardrobe* was computer-generated, including the main character of Aslan, creating and adding the computerised special effects took almost twice as long as the actual filming.

music
for Narnia

Music is an important medium for portraying emotion in a film. It sets the mood and enhances the action and the actors' performance. Traditionally stringed instruments are used for peaceful scenes while brash horn instruments might be used for a battle. The composer for *The Lion, the Witch and the Wardrobe* was Harry Gregson-Williams.

The music you hear in a movie is called the score and is composed to match the action on the screen. Once a film has been cut the director and editor meet with the composer for spotting sessions, where they view the film and discuss what kind of music should go where. Using this information the composer writes the music, or score, which is then recorded in scoring sessions.

The recording of a film score can be almost as complicated for the composer as making the film is for the director. The composer's trained ear and knowledge of music has to capture the emotional subtlety of the movie and translate it into music.

The process of recording the soundtrack takes place in an area with good acoustics and large enough to fit all the musicians and sometimes even a choir. Sitting behind glass in a recording booth, the sound engineers and mixers blend the sound and control the instrument volumes to achieve a balance that will enrich the viewing experience for the audience.

For the recording session the composer stands in front of multiple screens that show the action, and conducts the musicians in performing the section of the score he has written to accompany each particular scene.

The sounds of World War Two England and Narnia were used as the inspiration for a soundtrack that when mixed with visual and audio cues provides a full movie experience.

Publicity on a major feature film lasts throughout the length of the project, including pre-production (when a unit publicist begins setting the stage for publicity and press activities on the set during filming); production; and post-production (when studio staff publicists take over responsibility from the unit publicist, using advertising, movie trailers, the Internet, posters and magazines to promote the movie worldwide.

With very tight production schedules access for the media needs to be controlled. This is the job of the unit publicist, who balances the need to promote the movie and the production team's need to make it. The unit publicist for *The Lion, the Witch and the Wardrobe* was Ernie Malik, who became a mini-expert on the subject, so he could pitch the project to the press, providing them with background information.

One of his challenges was to keep the press interested when they couldn't visit the working set, so when an unusual angle came up, he made good use of it. Once when the ten wolves and their trainer had finished their work on the film, he allowed local press to visit them for interviews and pictures. This story was picked up nationally, on the Internet, and globally.

The Internet has created a new medium on which to promote films, although the publicist's job remains the same – pitch a story, host a set visit and monitor the coverage when it breaks in the media. Ernie also conducted spot interviews with cast and crew and worked with a video crew making a behind-the-scenes documentary, which will be part of the film's promotion, and recording material for the DVD which is released six months after the movie.

The job of a unit publicist happens on set (hosting visiting press observing filming and interviewing key cast and film makers); behind the scenes (spending four hours each day on the set); and in the production office (captioning photos taken by the set still photographer, writing publicity notes about the production and suggesting stories to the press via phone calls or Internet e-mails).

Above left
Ernie Malik with a cameraman from his EPK crew on set.

Above right
Phil Bray: 'I have a silencer for my camera for shooting during the takes, which helps the actors to forget you're there. You're a fly on the wall, but a good part of the wall where you can see the action. It's not like taking a photo of a sunset where you can come back the next day and try again if you made a mistake — you need to concentrate on what's going on and capture that, because once the scene is over, if you missed it — it's gone.'

publicity and promotion
of Narnia

The unit publicist writes career biographies of the key cast and crew and once filming gets under way, works with the assistant directors, scheduling actors' time for interviews during breaks in filming. The publicist also needs to look for story ideas, for example special wardrobe or make-up being designed for the film, and needs to develop a close relationship with key cast members, many of whom will be asked to do press interviews.

When you see an article in a magazine or newspaper and you see the film illustrated you are seeing a 'still' shot while filming was taking place. Phil Bray was the Unit Still Photographer for *The Lion, the Witch and the Wardrobe*, and his job was to provide photographic material for publicity and advertising. He stands beside the A camera and when they shoot a wide shot he does the same and if they shoot a tight shot so does he, shooting with the same-size lens and exposure so his photos will mimic what appears on film. His camera is put inside a 'blimp' which is a soundproof lead box when he is filming during shooting and he needs to be a fly on the wall so that the actors are not distracted.

Once the film has been edited his still photos of key scenes and characters are used for the press kit, poster art, illustrating books about the movie or for the DVD and video packaging. He also takes behind-the-scenes photos of the director and crew for press publicity.

Phil Bray (close centre) captures a scene with his still camera. When the camera is rolling Phil is there to capture the stills. He uses film but digital cameras are now being used as well. As the still images are a valuable commodity commercially there is tight security to ensure they don't fall into the wrong hands.

People can now watch DVDs of movies in their own homes. These can include material about how the movie was made, the key people involved and other interesting extra features. This is a fairly new phenomenon and has become particularly important in the last few years. The DVD crew document everything that happens on a movie set so when you buy the DVD there will be comprehensive documentaries covering every facet of production. DVDs give even the most casual viewer a richer understanding of their favourite movies.

The DVD production team for *The Lion, the Witch and the Wardrobe* used advanced video cameras with anamorphic lenses which distort the image when you shoot it and fit it on a square frame and unstretches it when you play it on a wide-screen TV.

The team shot over 1000 hours of footage, with three cameramen covering all facets of the movie, documenting the people creating 'the work', spending five weeks at Weta Workshop watching them make armour and swords.

While the DVD team is part of the crew, working for the studio, they have to maintain an outside observer status and be impartial. In a way the DVD is part of the history of the film's production, something that will document how the movie was made once the cast and crew have moved on to other projects. The people that make movies will pass on but the movie remains.

DVD producers hope to show the personalities involved in making movies. The audience think actors are larger than life because they see them on the movie screen and want to know what they're like when they're not playing a role. The DVD tries to show the reality — that they are people and not just legends who only live in celluloid and light.

the
movie
of the
movie
— taking Narnia to the world

acknowledgements

Watching films being made is a passion of mine. Being part of *The Lion, the Witch and the Wardrobe* has been a real privilege and one of the highlights of my life. This window into a world few get to see has only been made possible through the help and cooperation of many people.

I would especially like to thank Ernie Malik. He was my lifeline on set — he taught me the protocols and introduced me to the amazing group of people who have worked so hard to film Narnia.

My special thanks go to Andrew Adamson and his entire team. They put up with me poking a camera lens and a dictaphone into their intensive work routine and did it graciously and cooperatively. Disney and Walden Media have been brilliant. In particular I would like to thank Christine Cadena, who did so much to provide me with images of the finished movie.

Phil Bray was particularly generous — I spent a lot of time on his patch, which he coped with so patiently — and taught me so much.

Many thanks to Barbara O'Shannessy for transcribing many hours of interviews and my deepest appreciation to Graeme Ramshaw and the Trustees of the NZ Fighter Pilots Museum who allowed me time away from my day passion.

One of the pleasures has been seeing *The Lion, the Witch and the Wardrobe* brought to life. I would like to thank the CS Lewis Estate for granting me this privilege and for their foresight in allowing a classic of children's literature to become a classic movie.

Thanks also go to Landrover for providing me with land transportation to remote places and Crystal Cruises for giving me time to put all my thoughts into words.

One of the joys of these works is meeting people and making new friends. As well as all those I have made on set I have also had wonderful support from the entire team at HarperCollins. My editor Lorain Day is now a very good friend who knows how to put up with me.

Finally thanks to my family at home who have helped me in so many ways and put up with those many days away from home and then grunts and moans from the husband and father in his office. Thanks Dianne, Travis, Sally-Anne and Belinda.

Ian Brodie
Wanaka